This is MADNESZ

Martijn Derksen

BookLeaf
Publishing

India | USA | UK

Presentation by *BookLeaf Publishing*

Web: www.bookleafpub.com

E-mail: info@bookleafpub.com

ISBN: 978-93-5744-940-3

First edition 2022

DEDICATION

The One, Anyone & No-one

The Great I Am

My Grandmother Aleida, Dorry Arts and MJ

ACKNOWLEDGEMENT

You know who you are, you are special in my heart.

"Everything you bring, do it from within."

PREFACE

This collection of text has been 15 years or more in the making. Never before has it seen the public light of day. I hope you enjoy reading as much as I enjoyed bringing it together.

And remember, there is no genius without a touch of MADNESZ.

It's Okay

Hey, hey It's okay
But I'm not going to live this way

This way is
to make more money everyday

This way is
leading humanity astray

To dissolve this way
only requires attention to pay

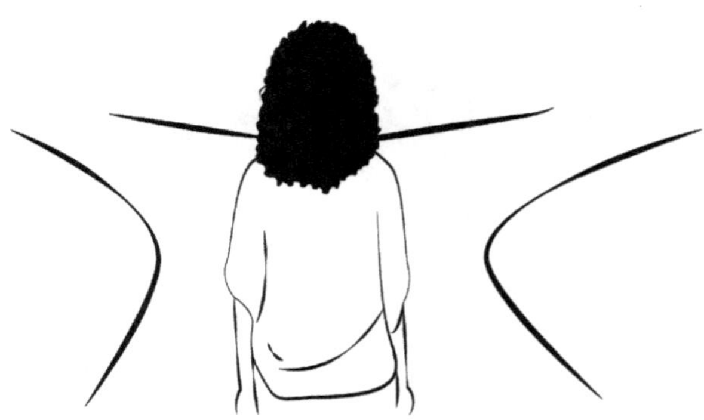

Stop the Debt Trap

Stop the debt trap
Stop the debt trap
It drives us mad

Live in freedom
Live in freedom
When the debt is gone

Plastic Soup

There is a coup
going on in our oceans

It's a plastic soup
going on in our oceans

A giant scoop
going on in our oceans

Reproduction is no Solution

More plastic pollution is no solution
More information doesn't help the nation
More we say is a neverending ratrace

Memorisation is no education
History is only one side of the story
Math can become a language of wrath

It's about what we do with what is given
More of the same, leads to scarcity and shame
The reproduction of the same old is putting us
on hold

We could learn to see the world anew
To see a solution in the morning dew

Now we are at this junction
'cause reproduction is no solution

The road not taken

You Think You Can Dominate Me

You think you can dominate me,
rule over me

You think you can,
but you cannot

Dominate me, rule over me
You think you can, but you cannot

Mother earth has spoken, now stop

Tell Every Boy and Girl

Tell every boy and every girl money no longer rules the world

Right on the clock of the universe, everything is going in reverse

We are in the midst of the greatest transformation for freedom in the history of every nation

Now Love

Right here on earth
You'll witness heaven's birth

Now love,
love like it's your very last day on earth
And live it like it's your very first

You can reach out your hand
or give a simple smile
to every person in your life

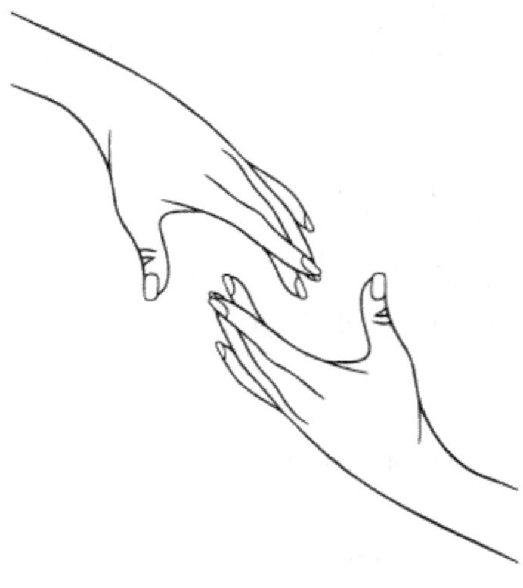

Love in our Hearts

Tonight we celebrate
stand fierce and radiate

No room for hate,
Let live and tolerate

We used to lay down low
That's not the way to go

Could you ever believe, we would succeed
Could we ever see, coming from the sixties
Dream to stand where we are, right now

With nothing, but
warm warm hearts

Don't stand still
Love live and walk the hill

Time to create
Wake up, don't hibernate

We used to lay down low
That's not the way to go

Could you ever believe, we would succeed
Could we ever see, coming from the sixties
Dream to stand where we are, right now

With nothing, but
Love is the start

Full of pride and joy
we're not here to destroy

Life's main thing
Is to dance and to sing

We used to lay down low
That's not the way to go

Could you ever believe, we would succeed
Could we ever see, coming from the sixties
Dream to stand where we are, right now

With nothing, but
Love in our Hearts

Free Humanity

We are here to heal the hearts
All you have to do, you see

Open up to everything you can be
Open hearts and minds

And humanity, you'll be free.
Free humanity. You will be free!

CARE

to Care or not to care
that's the whole switch right there

when we Ask why don't we care for mother,
you say don't bother

as long as the birds sing, nature knows,
we are on to do the Right thing

we are all on this Earth together
and we can all make this world a little better.

we are the sun, we are the stars,
the universe is what we are

Who is God?

People ask me who is God
I can only tell you what he's not

Keep your food, when you've have a lot
That's you, not God

You could have shared it in the name of love

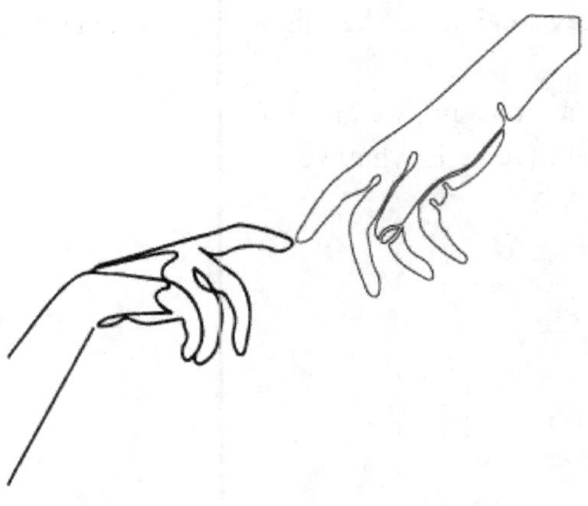

Matters of the Spirit

God is one. Always has been, always is and
always will be
No thing, nowhere and no one can separate this
oneness

This is the hidden at-onement
for every-one to be
even those who do not have eyes to see

This very moment Life is encouraging you to
see the oneness
feel the unity, be the undivided one

The matter of the spirit is that spirit matters
Everyone's spirit matters

You spirit, you matter

Change the world a little bit

People getting killed
People getting shot
And I don't know why

People getting banned
People getting scammed
Is it happening more and more?

Why, why, why
Why is the world like this
Can't you try to

Change the world a little bit
Change the world a little bit
Cause I know you don't like it like it is
Change the world a little bit
Find the one who once did
Change the world a little bit

I don't care who you are
I don't care what you do
I don't care how you look

I only wonder if you maybe should

Change the world a little bit
Change the world a little bit
Cause I know you don't like it like it is
Change the world a little bit
Find the one who once did
Change the world a little bit

Cause I know you can
and I know you are going to
You can change the world
Like no one else!

Change the world a little bit
Change the world a little bit
Cause I know you don't like it like it is
Change the world a little bit
Find the one who once did
Change the world a little bit

Change the world bit by bit

Return & Unlearn

Return, unlearn. You got the fire, you just have
to let it burn
Return, unlearn. You got the fire, you just have
to let it burn
Its bullshit, or bullseye. Is it truth or is it a lie

Return, unlearn. You got the fire, you just have
to let it burn
Return, unlearn. You got the fire, you just have
to let it burn

You've got to feel it inside,
your heart has no place to hide

Embrace Nature within and without
That's what return and unlearn is all about

That Natural State

Return to that natural state
No it's not too late

Return to that natural state
Know your life is not a waste

Return knowing
the new earth is growing

Return knowing
that's where we're going

Return knowing
awareness growing

The Gift of a Mindshift

Here we are on this blue dot
Everything is important, is it not?

Get ready for a mindshift
You'll be working through all that swift soulshit

You will feel lost and be adrift
You'll get through seeing life is actually one big
gift

We are on this blue dot
And everything's important, but actually it's not

Work Through Me

He, He, He works through me
He is leaning in to help you see

The fire starts
right in our hearts

Sometimes believing seems hard to do
A great divide and could it be true

She believes people should be free
She sees the whole world in unity

And here is the secret key
the hidden at-onement in diversity

Rebirth

Cause I learned to walk again
and I learned to talk again
and I learned to see
unity

Rebirth.
it's a new life
it's a new world
it's a new earth
Rebirth

To Live =

To learn   to love   is to live
To love   to live   is to learn
To live   to learn   is to love

To live is to forgive
To forgive is transformative
The truth is, it's transformative to live

Civilized

I guess the truth is we don't really care,
about all of them up and down there

Shut your eyes, turn off the light.
Say there is no dark side to all, what we call
civilized

As long as you are alive
You can choose to not just survive

To do something, to act, to be wise
To live to the fullest, to thrive

So, just come together now.
Stop talking about

And I will show you how
Just come together now

This delay is infectious
Why do we keep having this distrust

Madnessssss

Madness should not be the equivalent of faith.
Love should be the equivalent of faith. Although
sometimes some people say love is madness.

Everything you bring, do it from within.

Start with yourself, love and do well
Start with yourself, get out of your shelf

Start with yourself, spread the words and tell
Start with yourself, love and do well

Start with yourSelf

www.ingramcontent.com/pod-product-compliance
Lightning Source LLC
LaVergne TN
LVHW021334200726
843509LV00014B/2533